You Are Humongous:
Affirmation for Young Girls
By Kim Ruff Moore
Published by Ruff Moore Media Publishing
© 2024 Kim Ruff Moore
All rights reserved. No part of this book may be reproduced, distributed, or transmitted in any form or by any means, including photocopying, recording, or other electronic or mechanical methods, without the prior written permission of the publisher, except in the case of brief quotations embodied in critical reviews and certain other noncommercial uses permitted by copyright law. For permission requests, write to the publisher at the address below.
Ruff Moore Media Publishing
www.kimruffmoore.com
www.ruffmooremedia.com
Printed in the United States of America

ISBN:: :979-8-8693-9117-9
Cover design by Kim Ruff- Moore
more information about the author and her work, please
www.kimruffmoore.com.

## Table of Contents

Introduction

Self-Love and Acceptance

Body Image and Self-Respect

Academic Confidence

Peer Pressure and Authenticity

Social Media and Real Life

Personal Growth and Goals

Positive Relationships

Self-Care and Mental Health

Confidence and Self-Belief

Resilience and Strength

Positivity and Gratitude

Self-Compassion and Forgiveness

Ambition and Aspiration

Epilogue

A Final Word from Kim Ruff Moore

About the Author

# You Are Humongous:

## Affirmation For Young Girls

# by Kim Ruff Moore

You Are Humongous

Dear Amazing Young ladies,

Welcome to "You Are Humongous"—a book filled with powerful words of affirmation designed to remind you of your immense worth and potential. In these pages, "humongous" is a metaphor for the vastness of your value, strength, and uniqueness. Just as the word suggests something large and major, so too are you—an extraordinary individual whose worth far surpasses that of rubies, a true gem in this world.

As you navigate the exciting and sometimes challenging years of adolescence, it's important to remember that you are priceless. Your thoughts, feelings, and dreams matter deeply. This book serves as a daily reminder of your significance, offering affirmations to uplift you, build your confidence, and reinforce the belief that you are capable of achieving greatness.

Each affirmation in this book is crafted to empower you, helping you to embrace your true self and navigate the pressures of modern culture with grace and resilience. May these words be your guiding light, a source of strength and encouragement, and a constant reminder that you are humongous—majestic, magnificent, and immeasurably valuable.

With love and admiration,
Kim Ruff Moore

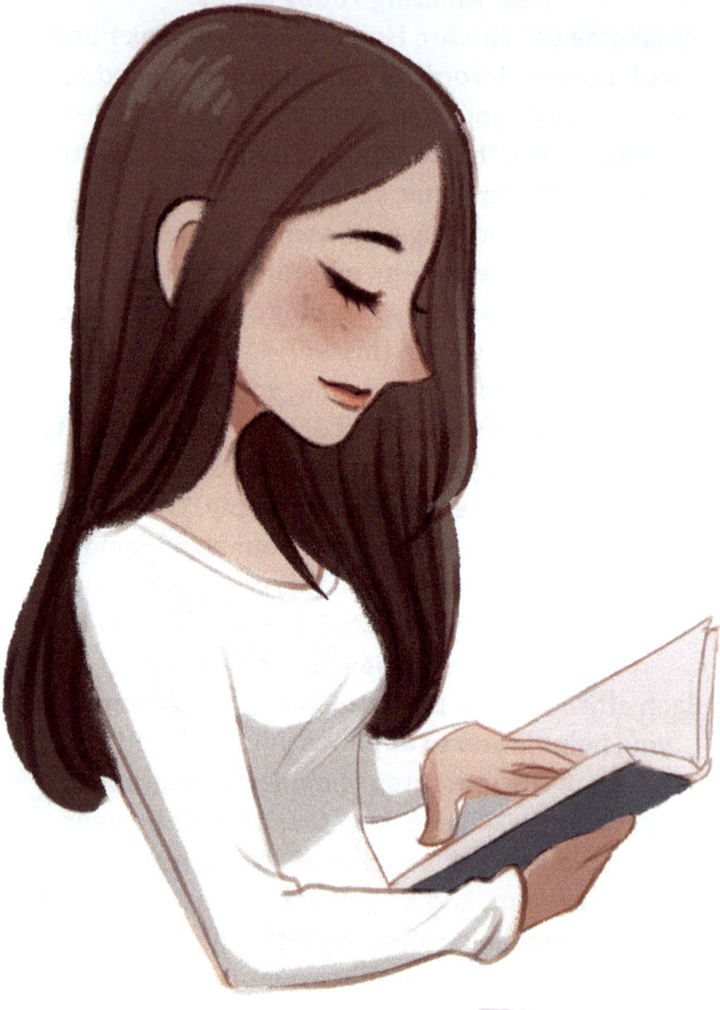

## *You Are Humongous!*

Welcome, Beautiful Soul
Your preteen and teenage years are a time of incredible growth and discovery. This journey can sometimes feel overwhelming, especially with the pressures of school, social media, and fitting in. But remember, you are unique, and your journey is your own. This book of positive affirmations is here to remind you of your worth, strength, and beauty. Let's embark on this journey together and fill your heart and mind with positivity and self-love.

## *You Are Humongous!*

**Embrace Your Uniqueness
You are one of a kind, and that's your superpower. Embrace everything that makes you different, for these are the traits that set you apart from the rest. Celebrate your quirks, your talents, and your personality.**

- **"I am proud of who I am becoming."**
- **"I love and accept myself exactly as I am."**
- **"My uniqueness is my strength."**

# You Are Humongous!

## *You Are Humongous!*

**Words Have Power**
**The way you speak to yourself matters. Practice positive self-talk daily. Replace negative thoughts with encouraging ones. You are your biggest cheerleader.**

- **"I am capable of achieving great things."**
- **"Every challenge I face is an opportunity to grow."**
- **"I believe in my abilities and my potential."**

## *You Are Humongous!*

### Love Your Body

Your body is amazing just the way it is. It carries you through life, and it deserves your love and respect. Focus on what your body can do, not just how it looks.

- "My body is beautiful and strong."
- "I nourish my body with healthy food and positive thoughts."
- "I appreciate all that my body does for me."

# You Are Humongous!

## *You Are Humongous!*

**Caring for Yourself Developing healthy habits is a form of self-love. Take care of your body and mind through balanced nutrition, regular exercise, and adequate rest.**

**"I treat my body with kindness and care."**

**"Healthy habits make me feel my best."**

**"I deserve to feel healthy and vibrant."**

## *You Are Humongous!*

**Value Your Education Education is a powerful tool that opens doors to countless opportunities. Embrace learning and believe in your ability to succeed academically.**

- **"I am capable of learning and growing."**
- **"I am dedicated to my education and my future."**
- **"I handle academic challenges with confidence and resilience**

## *You Are Humongous!*

## You Can Do It

Every academic challenge is an opportunity to develop resilience and problem-solving skills. Believe in your ability to overcome obstacles and keep pushing forward.

- "I am smart and capable."
- "Challenges help me grow stronger and wiser."
- "I am persistent and determined in my studies."

# *You Are Humongous!*

## *You Are Humongous!*

### Stay True to Yourself

Peer pressure can be tough, but staying true to who you are is crucial. Your values and beliefs matter, and they make you who you are.

- "I trust myself to make the right decisions."
- "I stay true to my values and beliefs."
- "I am confident in my choices and who I am."

You Are Humorous!

## *You Are Humongous!*

## You Are Strong

You have the strength to resist peer pressure and make choices that align with your true self. Surround yourself with people who respect and support you.

- "I am strong enough to stand up for myself."
- "I choose friends who respect me for who I am."
- "I am confident in my ability to make good choices."

## *You Are Humongous!*

## Navigating Social Media
Social media can be fun, but it's important to remember that it's just a highlight reel of people's lives. Focus on real-life connections and experiences.

- "I am more than my social media presence."
- "I value real-life connections over online appearances."
- "I use social media mindfully and positively."

## *You Are Humongous!*

Understanding and affirming your worth is crucial for self-love and acceptance. Your worth is not determined by others but by your own intrinsic value.

- "I am worthy of love and respect."
- "I bring value to the world around me."
- "My worth is not defined by external factors."
- "I am deserving of happiness and success."
- "I value myself and my contributions."

# You Are Humongous!

## *You Are Humongous!*

Individuality is what makes each person special. Celebrate your individuality by acknowledging and embracing what makes you different.

- "I celebrate my individuality."
- "I am unique and that is my strength."
- "I honor my own path and journey."
- "I bring a unique perspective to the world."
- "I am confident in my own skin."

## *You Are Humongous!*

Developing healthy habits is a form of self-love. Take care of your body and mind through balanced nutrition, regular exercise, and adequate rest.

- "I make healthy choices for my body."
- "Exercise makes me feel strong and energized."
- "I choose foods that nourish and fuel me."
- "Rest is essential, and I give myself permission to relax."
- "I listen to my body's needs."

# *You Are Humongous!*

## *You Are Humongous!*

Developing healthy habits is a form of self-love. Take care of your body and mind through balanced nutrition, regular exercise, and adequate rest.

- "I make healthy choices for my body."
- "Exercise makes me feel strong and energized."
- "I choose foods that nourish and fuel me."
- "Rest is essential, and I give myself permission to relax."
- "I listen to my body's needs."

## *You Are Humongous!*

Self-respect is about valuing yourself and your boundaries. Treat yourself with the same respect you offer to others.

- "I respect myself and my boundaries."
- "I deserve to be treated with kindness and respect."
- "I stand up for myself and my values."
- "I make choices that honor my well-being."
- "I am worthy of respect and dignity."

# You Are Humongous!

## *You Are Humongous!*

Every academic challenge is an opportunity to develop resilience and problem-solving skills. Believe in your ability to overcome obstacles and keep pushing forward.

- "I am smart and capable."
- "Challenges help me grow stronger and wiser."
- "I am persistent and determined in my studies."
- "I find solutions to the problems I face."
- "I learn from my mistakes and improve."

# *You Are Humongous!*

## *You Are Humongous!*

**Developing Study Habits**
Good study habits are key to academic success. Create a productive study environment and stick to a schedule that works for you.

- "I am disciplined in my study habits."
- "I create a study routine that works for me."
- "I stay organized and manage my time well."
- "I seek help when I need it."
- "I am focused and dedicated to my studies."

## *You Are Humongous!*

**Balancing Academics and Life Finding a balance between academics and personal life is essential for overall well-being. Make time for relaxation, hobbies, and social activities.**

- **"I balance my academic and personal life well."**
- **"I make time for rest and relaxation."**
- **"I enjoy my hobbies and interests outside of school."**
- **"I prioritize my mental and physical health."**
- **"I am successful in both my studies and personal life."**

*You Are Humongous!*

## *You Are Humongous!*

**Stay True to Yourself**

Peer pressure can be tough, but staying true to who you are is crucial. Your values and beliefs matter, and they make you who you are.

- "I trust myself to make the right decisions."
- "I stay true to my values and beliefs."
- "I am confident in my choices and who I am."
- "I do not need to conform to fit in."
- "I respect myself and my choices."

# *You Are Humongous!*

## Handling Peer Pressure

You have the strength to resist peer pressure and make choices that align with your true self. Surround yourself with people who respect and support you.

- "I am strong enough to stand up for myself."
- "I choose friends who respect me for who I am."
- "I am confident in my ability to make good choices."
- "I say no to things that don't align with my values."
- "I seek out positive and supportive relationships."

# *You Are Humongous!*

## *You Are Humongous!*

Authentic relationships are built on trust, respect, and mutual support. Focus on building meaningful connections with others.

- "I build relationships based on trust and respect."
- "I surround myself with positive and supportive people."
- "I am a good friend and attract good friends."
- "I communicate openly and honestly with others."
- "I value quality over quantity in my friendships."

# *You Are Humongous!*

## *You Are Humongous!*

### Being Your True Self

Being authentic means being true to who you are, even when it's difficult. Embrace your true self and let it shine.

- "I am proud of who I am."
- "I embrace my true self and let it shine."
- "I do not need to change to please others."
- "I am confident in my uniqueness."
- "I celebrate my individuality and authenticity."

# *You Are Humongous!*

**Real vs. Online Persona**
**Understand the difference between real life and online personas. What you see online is often curated and doesn't reflect the whole picture.**

- "I understand that social media is not real life."
- "I do not compare my real life to others' highlight reels."
- "I focus on being authentic both online and offline."
- "I prioritize real-life experiences and connections."
- "I recognize the difference between reality and online images."

# You Are Humongous!

## *You Are Humongous!*

**Setting Social Media Boundaries**
Setting boundaries around social media use is crucial for mental health. Limit your time online and be mindful of what you consume.

- "I set healthy boundaries for social media use."
- "I take breaks from social media to recharge."
- "I curate my feed to include positive and inspiring content."
- "I do not let social media dictate my self-worth."
- "I use social media in a balanced and healthy way."

# *You Are Humongous!*

**Positive Online Interactions**
Engage in positive and uplifting interactions online. Spread kindness and support, and avoid negative or toxic environments.

- "I spread kindness and positivity online."
- "I engage in uplifting and supportive interactions."
- "I avoid negative and toxic online environments."
- "I report and block harmful content and behavior."
- "I use my online presence to make a positive impact."

# *You Are Humongous!*

# *You Are Humongous!*

**Setting and Achieving Goals**
**Setting goals gives you direction and purpose. Break down your goals into manageable steps and celebrate your progress along the way.**

- "I set clear and achievable goals."
- "I take small steps towards my big dreams."
- "I celebrate my progress and achievements."
- **"I stay motivated and focused on my goals."**
- "I believe in my ability to achieve

## *You Are Humongous!*

**Visualizing Success**
**Visualization is a powerful tool for achieving your goals. Picture yourself succeeding and feel the emotions associated with that success.**

- "I visualize my success and take steps to achieve it."
- "I see myself reaching my goals and celebrate the journey."
- "I use positive visualization to motivate and inspire me."
- "I imagine the best version of myself and work towards it."
- "I trust that my hard work and dedication will pay off."

# You Are Humongous!

# *You Are Humongous!*

**Adapting to Change**
**Change is a natural part of life. Embrace it as an opportunity to grow and learn.**

- **"I embrace change and see it as an opportunity to grow."**
- **"I am adaptable and open to new experiences."**
- **"I trust myself to navigate through change with grace."**
- **"I welcome new opportunities that come my way."**
- **"I am resilient and can handle change positively."**

## *You Are Humongous!*

**Cultivating a Growth Mindset**
A growth mindset allows you to see challenges as opportunities for growth. Believe in your ability to develop and improve.

- "I have a growth mindset and embrace challenges."
- "I learn from my experiences and improve continuously."
- "I am not afraid to fail, as it is a part of my growth."
- "I seek out opportunities to learn and grow."
- "I believe in my capacity to learn and develop."

# You Are Humongous!

# *You Are Humongous!*

**Building Supportive Friendships**
Healthy friendships are based on mutual respect, support, and understanding. Surround yourself with people who lift you up.

- "I attract positive and supportive friends."
- "I am a loyal and caring friend."
- "I build relationships based on trust and respect."
- "I choose friends who encourage and support me."
- "I am grateful for the amazing friends in my life."

## *You Are Humongous!*

**Family Dynamics**

Family relationships can be complex, but they are also a source of support and love. Focus on building strong connections with your family members.

"I appreciate and love my family."
"I communicate openly and honestly with my family."
"I am patient and understanding with my family members."
"I contribute to a positive and loving family environment."
"I value the support and love of my family."

# *You Are Humongous!*

## *You Are Humongous!*

## Healthy Boundaries
Setting healthy boundaries is crucial for maintaining positive relationships. Respect yourself and ensure others respect you too.

- "I set and maintain healthy boundaries."
- "I respect myself and expect the same from others."
- "I communicate my needs and boundaries clearly."
- "I do not feel guilty for setting boundaries."
- "I surround myself with people who respect my boundaries.

## *You Are Humongous!*

**Resolving Conflicts**

Conflicts are a natural part of relationships. Learn to address and resolve them in a healthy and constructive way.

- "I handle conflicts with patience and understanding."
- "I listen actively and communicate clearly during conflicts."
- "I seek solutions that are fair and respectful to all involved."
- "I learn from conflicts and grow stronger."
- "I maintain respect and kindness even in disagreements."

# *You Are Humongous!*

## *You Are Humongous!*

**Importance of Self-Care**
**Self-care is essential for your overall well-being. Make time for activities that nourish your body, mind, and soul.**

- **"I prioritize self-care and make time for myself."**
- **"I listen to my body and mind's needs."**
- **"I engage in activities that bring me joy and relaxation."**
- **"I take care of my mental and physical health."**
- **"I deserve to feel rested and rejuvenated."**

# *You Are Humongous!*

## *You Are Humongous!*

**Seeking Help When Needed**
It's okay to ask for help when you need it. Reaching out is a sign of strength, not weakness.

- "I am not afraid to ask for help when I need it."
- "I seek support from trusted friends, family, or professionals."
- "I take proactive steps to care for my mental health."
- "I am strong for recognizing when I need support."
- "I am worthy of help and support."

## *You Are Humongous!*

**Mindfulness and Relaxation Practicing mindfulness and relaxation techniques can help reduce stress and improve your overall well-being.**

- "I practice mindfulness to stay present and grounded."
- "I find peace and relaxation in the present moment."
- "I use breathing exercises to calm my mind and body."
- "I engage in activities that help me relax and unwind."
- "I am at peace with myself and my surroundings."

# You Are Humongous!

## *You Are Humongous!*

**Emotional Well-Being**
Taking care of your emotional health is just as important as your physical health. Allow yourself to feel and process your emotions.

- "I acknowledge and honor my emotions."
- "I allow myself to feel and express my emotions."
- "I take time to understand and process my feelings."
- "I am in tune with my emotional well-being."
- "I nurture my emotional health with care and compassion."

*You Are Humongous!*

## *You Are Humongous!*

**Empowerment and Future Vision Empower yourself and visualize a positive and fulfilling future. Believe in your ability to shape your destiny.**

- **"I am in control of my own destiny."**
- **"I have the power to create a positive future."**
- **"I believe in my ability to achieve my dreams."**
- **"I am confident in my path and my potential."**
- **"I look forward to a bright and fulfilling future."**

# You Are Humongous!

## *You Are Humongous!*

**Confidence and Self-Belief Believing in yourself is the foundation for all your achievements. Confidence comes from within and is built by acknowledging your strengths and embracing your journey.**

- "I believe in myself and my abilities."
- "I am confident in my skills and talents."
- "I trust myself to make the right decisions."
- "I am proud of how far I have come."
- "I am brave, bold, and beautiful."

## *You Are Humongous!*

**Resilience and Strength**
Life's challenges are opportunities to build resilience. You have the strength to overcome obstacles and grow from your experiences.

- "I am resilient and can overcome any challenge."
- "Every setback is a setup for a comeback."
- "I grow stronger with every difficulty I face."
- "I am capable of handling whatever comes my way."
- "I turn challenges into opportunities for growth."

*re Humongous!*

# *You Are Humongous!*

**Positivity and Gratitude**
**A positive mindset and a heart filled with gratitude can transform your life. Focus on the good and be thankful for your blessings.**

- "I choose to focus on the positive in every situation."
- "I am grateful for all the good things in my life."
- "I radiate positivity and attract good things."
- "I find joy in the simple things."
- "I am thankful for each new day and the opportunities it brings."

## *You Are Humongous!*

**Self-Compassion and Forgiveness Being kind to yourself is essential for your well-being. Practice self-compassion and forgive yourself for past mistakes.**

- "I am gentle and compassionate with myself."
- "I forgive myself for my mistakes and learn from them."
- "I am patient with myself as I grow and change."
- "I deserve my own kindness and respect."
- "I am proud of my progress and growth."

# You Are Humongous!

## *You Are Humongous!*

**Ambition and Aspiration
Dream big and aim high. Your ambitions are valid, and you have the power to turn them into reality. Stay focused and keep striving.**

- "I am ambitious and driven."
- "I set high goals and work hard to achieve them."
- "I believe in my potential to succeed."
- "I am focused and determined to reach my dreams."
- "I am unstoppable and destined for greatness."

# *You Are Humongous!*

Dear Reader,

As you close this book of affirmations, I want to remind you that the journey of self-discovery and self-love is a continuous one. You have taken a significant step by embracing these affirmations and allowing them to nurture your mind and soul. Each affirmation is a seed planted in the fertile soil of your heart, ready to blossom into confidence, strength, and unwavering self-belief.

Your teenage years are a time of incredible growth, filled with both challenges and triumphs. It is a period where you are discovering who you are and what you stand for. Remember, it is perfectly okay to feel uncertain and to make mistakes. These experiences are integral to your journey, shaping you into the remarkable individual you are destined to become.

In a world obsessed with aesthetics, designer clothes, and social media personas, it is easy to lose sight of what truly matters. But know this: your worth is not determined by your appearance, your wardrobe, or the number of likes you receive. Your worth is intrinsic, unchanging, and infinite. It is found in your kindness, your intelligence, your resilience, and your capacity for love.

Every affirmation in this book is a testament to your inner strength and beauty. They are reminders that you are capable, you are enough, and you are deserving of all the good things life has to offer. Carry these affirmations with you as you navigate through school, friendships, and the pressures of modern culture. Let them be your anchor in times of doubt and your light in moments of darkness.

I hope that as you read and repeat these affirmations, you come to realize just how extraordinary you are. I hope you see yourself through the lens of compassion and understanding, and that you treat yourself with the same kindness you so readily offer to others.

Believe in your dreams, cherish your uniqueness, and never forget that you have the power to shape your future. Surround yourself with people who uplift and support you, and never be afraid to stand up for who you are and what you believe in.

Thank you for allowing me to be a part of your journey. I am incredibly proud of the person you are and the person you are becoming. Keep these affirmations close, revisit them often, and let them guide you towards a life filled with joy, purpose, and unwavering self-love.

With all my love and support,
Kim Ruff Moore

# *You Are Humongous!*

# About The Author

Kim Ruff Moore is a multifaceted artist whose talents have touched hearts across the globe. As a Stellar Award-winning singer-songwriter and national recording artist, Kim's voice carries messages of hope and inspiration.

Beyond her musical achievements, Kim has established herself as a prolific author with an impressive repertoire of 35 published books. Her works span various genres, from children's literature to insightful guides on finances and relationships. Kim's dedication to uplifting others is evident in the five-star ratings her books consistently receive.

A champion of literacy, Kim has created several beloved book series for children, including "Suzzie Moch," "Spence Seven," "Sergio the Studio Mouse," "Kirby the Koala," and "Harper Sharper," among others. Through imaginative storytelling, Kim instills valuable lessons and fosters creativity in young minds.

Kim's creative endeavors extend beyond the written word. She is a proud member of the duo group "The New Consolers," alongside her husband, Jeffrey Moore, who is a renowned music producer with roots in the legendary Sam Cooke band. Jeffrey's induction into the DooWap Hall of Fame in 2013 is a testament to his musical legacy. Together, Kim and Jeffrey captivate audiences worldwide with their soul-stirring performances. Their shared passion for music and storytelling creates an unforgettable experience for listeners of all ages.

In addition to her artistic pursuits, Kim generously shares her literary platform at various functions and speaking engagements, inspiring others to pursue their passions and fulfill their potential.

Kim and Jeffrey's family life is equally enriching, with four children who undoubtedly inherit their parents' creativity and drive. Their son Spencer, also a writer, serves as the inspiration behind the acclaimed "Spence Seven" book series, continuing the family's legacy of storytelling and inspiration.

Through her music, writing, and advocacy, Kim Ruff Moore continues to make a profound impact, spreading joy and empowerment wherever her talents take her.

Milton Keynes UK
Ingram Content Group UK Ltd.
UKHW020720050624
443487UK00010B/18